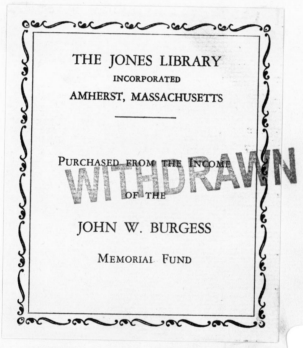

William Zorach

JOHN I. H. BAUR

WILLIAM

Published for the WHITNEY MUSEUM OF AMERICAN ART

ZORACH

by Frederick A. Praeger, *Publishers,* New York, 1959

730.923

BIBLIOGRAPHY BY Rosalind Irvine
Curator, Whitney Museum of American Art.

BOOKS THAT MATTER Published in the United States of America in 1959 by Frederick A. Praeger, Inc.,
Publishers. 15 West 47th Street, New York 36, N. Y.
Library of Congress catalogue card number 59-10500.
Copyright © 1959 by the Whitney Museum of American Art.
Designed by Peter Oldenburg. Printed in the United States of America.

Foreword and Acknowledgments

This book grew out of a retrospective exhibition of William Zorach's sculpture, paintings, watercolors and drawings held at the Whitney Museum of American Art in the fall of 1959. It contains, however, a much fuller account of his life and work and many more illustrations than the catalogue of that exhibition.

In the course of a long career, which has won him an eminent position in the world of American art, Zorach has been active in many fields. In addition to his own work, he has taught both the practice and history of sculpture, has lectured widely, written numerous books and articles and a sizeable body of unpublished poetry. I am most grateful to him for making available all his manuscripts, notes, letters, clippings and biographical material relating to these and his other activities, the majority of which had fortunately just been catalogued and put into chronological order by the Archives of American Art. Miss Bartlett Cowdrey, its Archivist in the New York area, was most helpful in this respect. Both the artist and his wife have also been extremely kind in answering a multitude of questions, in putting the contents of the studio at my disposal, in having many works photographed which had not been reproduced before, and in more ways than I can hope to acknowledge here.

This book could scarcely have been written without the generous assistance of The Downtown Gallery, which has been Zorach's dealer for some thirty years. Its admirably complete records of his work, its kindness in supplying information and photographs, and its cooperation in every stage of this undertaking were of inestimable help. I am most grateful to its director, Mrs. Edith Gregor Halpert, to John C. Marin, Jr. and to Lawrence Allen.

I am greatly indebted to an earlier book on the artist, Paul S. Wingert's *The Sculpture of William Zorach,* published in 1938. His excellent catalogue raisonné of work done up to that time was most useful, and there is little that one can add to his appraisal of Zorach's early career. I must also acknowledge the kindness of the Carnegie Study of the Arts of the United States and the personal help of Lamar Dodd and Charles B. Phelps in making available the color transparencies for all of the color plates in these pages except that of *The Future Generation,* which was photographed by Oliver Baker.

I owe a special debt of gratitude to two of my colleagues at the Whitney Museum: Miss Rosalind Irvine, Curator, who compiled the bibliography and index and Mrs. Edwin Westlake who not only typed the manuscript but handled efficiently so much of the organization of both book and exhibition.

Finally I would like to thank the many private collectors and museums who made their sculptures by Zorach available for the exhibition and permitted them to be reproduced here. They are unfortunately too numerous to be listed in this foreword, but their names appear beneath the illustrations of their works.

J.I.H.B.

Measurements in the captions are in inches unless otherwise noted. Height precedes width except in the case of sculpture, where the largest dimension is given.

William Zorach

In his seventy-two years William Zorach has made two long journeys: one from the obscurity of a poor Lithuanian immigrant to a position of fame (and reasonable prosperity) in American art, the other from a youthful partisan in the revolutionary cause of modernism to a mature traditionalist upholding that most ancient concept of sculpture as a hewn image.

Perhaps the most significant thing about these two journeys is the fact that they are unrelated. It was not for fame's sake that Zorach turned, at a crucial moment in his life, toward a more conservative ideal. Nor was it the natural conservatism of age—that unwillingness to struggle longer with a new form of expression, which he himself described, in the remote days of 1921, when he wrote, "For many it is too great a task. Some go back, richer for their travels and explorations into the unknown. Others stop altogether and take up work along lines of lesser resistance."[1]

In Zorach's case it was none of these things. The change in his art and in his attitude was dictated more by instinct than conscious choice. Gradually he became aware that everything he felt most deeply in life was an inextricable mixture of physical and spiritual elements—the grace of animals, the attraction of man and woman, the tenderness of motherhood—primitive facts of being, but universal ones. At the same time he discovered that carving was, for him at least, the natural means of expressing these underlying tides of life. The very slowness of the process, the amplitude of emerging forms, the massive movement, the strong and simple relation of parts in a harmonious whole created esthetic equivalents to the themes that moved him without being literal transcriptions of them. For a brief span he struggled to accommodate his earlier faith in the absolute primacy of design to his growing need for a closer relationship to nature. There was no one moment of decision, but there was a day still remembered, in the early 1920's, when the whole of modernism seemed suddenly too cerebral, a day when he consciously resolved to forget theory and to trust the validity of his own vision. His finest sculpture came thereafter.

So there has been a kind of paradox in Zorach's career, though an understandable one. The further he has moved from his Baltic peasant background, the more clearly his art has reflected its response to life's enduring cycle on the most direct physical and emotional level. It was the young immigrant, just emerged from the alien section of Cleveland's poor, who embraced the sophistication of fauvism and cubism. It is the older and more truly sophisticated artist who has recognized that his own source of strength lies, like that of Antaeus, closer to the earth.

The ancestral earth, in Zorach's case, was Eurburg, Lithuania, where he was born on February 28, 1887, the seventh of ten children. His memory of it is fragmentary, since he was only four when he was brought to America, but the stories told by his mother are still vivid in his mind. "My father sailed a freight barge up the Niemen River from Königsberg to Rovno," he wrote in a letter many years later. "We used to spend the summers on the barge, a small affair that floated down the river and [was] dragged and sailed upstream. Once in a while one of us would fall overboard and almost drown. My oldest sister was caught by her long golden locks just as she went down for the third time. Before I was born, many years ago, Cossacks used to raid the villages and snatch little boys for the army. So my uncle, then a small boy, stole away to America. He worked here for many years, carrying a pack on his back from farmhouse to farmhouse selling needle notions, etc. After many years he sent for his brother, my father, who came first with my oldest brother. They worked and struggled to save enough to send for my mother and the rest of the family, but it was hard. One day my father found five brand new five-dollar bills on the country road which he was tramping, which helped to pay our passage.

"Of Russia I only remember a low log cabin with mud floors and a huge oven upon which we slept cold nights. I remember the clanking of the chains as they let the stage pass over the border when we crossed into Germany on our way to America, and I remember almost falling out of the porthole on the huge ship that brought us to America. My mother landed in New York without one penny, and on the train to Cleveland a vendor passed a box of candy to the passengers and my mother thought what a beautiful country, but when he came back to collect she had no money so had to sell a silver spoon to one of the passengers to pay for the candy."

For three years the reunited family lived at Port Clinton, Ohio, in a ramshackle house by the railroad, meagerly supported by Zorach's father, who now peddled his wares from a horse and wagon. Things were a little better in Cleveland, where they moved in 1894. His mother borrowed $300 and bought a house from an old man who continued to live with them as a boarder. His father established himself in the junk business while the young Zorach earned his first money selling newspapers. When he was thirteen their finances remained so precarious that he quit school for a year and worked at a variety of jobs in a machine shop, a hat factory, a brass factory and carrying satchels for drummers.

Fortunately he returned to school (in the seventh grade), where the supervisor, recognizing his exceptional talent as a draftsman, recommended that he learn the trade of a lithographer and study nights at the

1. SPRING, NUMBER 1. 1913. Oil. 40 x 46. The Downtown Gallery.

Cleveland School of Art. This was essentially the program which Zorach
followed. His academic education ended with the eighth grade, and in
1902 he took a job as errand boy, at three dollars a week, with the Morgan
Lithograph Company. From 1903 to 1906 he was apprenticed to the same
firm, working his first year at no salary, then at a wage which rose slowly
to seven dollars a week. But at the end he knew his trade thoroughly
and for many years thereafter he supported himself as a journeyman
lithographer. During the same period he spent his evenings at the Cleveland School of Art, drawing and painting. His interest in sculpture was
not to awaken for some time, but it was here that he determined to
become an artist and to escape the commercialism of lithography as soon
as possible.

2. THE ROOF PLAYGROUND. 1917. Oil. 29 x 23¾. Collection of Tessim Zorach.

By 1907 Zorach had saved $160. With this modest capital he came to New York, slept for his first winter in a clothes closet provided by the cousin of a Cleveland friend, and began his two years of study at the art school of the National Academy of Design, where he eventually won a medal for drawing and an honorable mention in painting. Summers he returned to Cleveland and to his lithographer's job, which enabled him to move to more comfortable quarters. His spare time was spent at the public library, poring over reproductions of drawings by Holbein, Dürer, Ingres, and at the Metropolitan Museum copying old masters. Alternately working and studying (with a brief stint under George Bridgman at the Art Students League), he again contrived to save enough for the next step, a trip to France.

In 1910, at the age of 23, Zorach arrived in Paris, speaking scarcely a word of French. This proved something of an obstacle in his studies. After trying a number of schools, he finally settled on La Palette, largely because Jacques Emile Blanche gave his criticisms in English. John Duncan Fergusson also taught there and had, Zorach believes, more influence than any other teacher on his early development. More important, however, was his meeting with another young American student at La Palette, Marguerite Thompson, who was later to become his wife. She had been in France since 1906, had seen the birth of the cubist and fauve movements, and was already painting "wild" pictures herself. Zorach was partially converted, although the dominant influences on his art at this time were the more conservative forerunners of modernism, Cézanne, van Gogh and Gauguin. He spent the summer of 1911 sketching in the south of France and sent five of his own wild pictures to the Salon d'Automne where four were accepted.

Late in 1911 Zorach returned to America penniless, worked once more as a lithographer in Cleveland, and there exhibited for the first time in this country in the Taylor Galleries on the fourth floor of the department store, William Taylor Sons and Company—an event which netted him fifteen dollars in sales. But he was putting aside all he could of his earnings. "Within the year I had saved twelve hundred dollars—Marguerite had three hundred dollars. We met in New York [in December, 1912], went down to City Hall, were married, got ourselves a studio [at 55th Street and Sixth Avenue]. Canvas and paint we had brought from Paris, furniture we picked up anywhere we could find or borrow it, and red, blue and yellow obliterated its origin. We painted our floors with red lead, and decorated our walls with murals. We were modern (wildly modern) in days when a mere handful of people in America even knew Cubists and Fauves existed. We were drunk with the possibilities of color and form, and the new world that they opened up."[2]

They both had paintings in the Armory Show of 1913, but in that immense catch-all, with its more startling entries from Paris, their work received little notice. In the same year, however, Zorach was one of eight artists who banded together in a group exhibition at the MacDowell Club, and his picture, *The Red Sea*, appears to have been a storm center of the show. One newspaper critic, whose shocked reactions are preserved in an unidentified clipping, not only objected to the sea itself being red, but felt that the figures were "such strange types that we doubt if any of their antetypes of the present day would care to claim them. Some of the women have green skins and some pink, and one unfortunate pink woman has bright green hair."

To this and like reviews Zorach replied indirectly when he was invited to take part in the Forum Exhibition of 1916 with the other leading rebels of American art. "It is the inner spirit of things that I seek to express," he wrote in the catalogue, "the essential relations of forms and colors to universal things. Each form and color has a spiritual significance to me, and I try to combine these forms and colors within my space to express that inner feeling which something in nature or life has given me." His work of this period, roughly 1913-16, was markedly fauve in character and strongly influenced by Matisse, as the canvas *Spring, Number 1* (fig. 1) testifies. But despite its high key, its decorative patterning, its disregard of anatomical realism and strident chords of pink, blue, green and orange, the painting is, as Zorach himself remarked, more closely related to nature and thus essentially more conservative than the work of the French master. He must have had this picture in mind when he wrote in the same catalogue, "In the spring one feels the freshness of growing things, the ascending rhythm of life, the expanding of leaves and trees. . . . One feels the relation of the forms of birds, flowers, animals, trees, of everything that grows and breathes to each other and to the earth and sky." Like so many other young American modernists of these early years, Zorach instinctively adapted the more extreme concept of art as a language of pure form and color to the tradition of romantic naturalism in which he had been trained.

Even when, about 1917, he was impelled towards a still more radical dislocation of nature and abandoned fauvism for cubism, one senses a certain disparity between theory and practice in his art. Theoretically he subscribed with enthusiasm to the cubist credo. "The modern movement has freed art from the idea of reproducing nature," he wrote, "an idea which has been persistently followed since the Greeks and which has been suddenly found to have nothing to do with art. The *essential contribution* of modern art to aesthetics is the building and development of purely abstract forms and colors."[3] Actually, his pictures have none of the cerebral qualities of French cubism, nor do they deal with the same emotionally neutral subject matter. Instead, they interpret easily recognizable events and themes which moved the artist, and they are filled with a warmth of sentiment totally alien to pure abstraction. His wife and his own children—a son Tessim and a daughter Dahlov were born in 1915 and 1917 respectively—were often his subjects, and even in their cubist garb they are charged with tenderness, with gaiety and, as the title of one painting indicates, with adoration. Some of this feeling reached even the anonymous critic who described Zorach's *New England Family* in 1918 as "a cubistic mother feeding a geometrical baby out of a trigonometrical bottle," but reluctantly admitted that it gave him a true sense of its subject.

Today the best of these cubist works, such as the *Leo Ornstein* (fig. 4), *Interior and Exterior* (fig. 3) or *Mirage—Ships at Night* (fig. 5), are still impressive for their skillful handling of design and for their romantic content. The trouble is that the two elements are not always wedded with that inevitability which a durable art demands; the design, for all its skill, seems applied rather than organic. It was only in 1920, near the end of his career as a painter in oil, that Zorach hit briefly but with brilliant effect on a semi-abstract style which was more thoroughly

3. INTERIOR AND EXTERIOR. 1918. Oil. 36 x 28. The Downtown Gallery.

4. LEO ORNSTEIN—PIANO CONCERT. 1918. Oil. 30 x 24. The Downtown Gallery.

integrated with his aims and more truly personal in character. This was in the little known series of drawings, watercolors and a few oils which he executed in the Yosemite valley during that summer (figs. 7-12). In these the artist abandoned the paraphernalia of cubism—its angularities, dislocations and multiple views—in favor of a fluid handling which caught the essential lines and motion of the landscape, simplified them in a kind of decorative shorthand and wove them together into handsome designs marked by a dynamic play of light and heavy accents, of sweeping linear passages and irregular shapes. These pictures are quite unlike any European prototype; if anything they suggest rather the kind of nature-oriented abstraction which Georgia O'Keeffe and Arthur G. Dove were developing independently at the same time. But in any case they are entirely personal to Zorach and stand out today as the most interesting graphic work of his career.

For two more years Zorach continued to think of himself as a painter, although he had already begun to carve. In his last oils he returned to a more modified cubism, closer to Cézanne than to Picasso, and abandoned the direction of his Yosemite works as abruptly as he had begun it (fig. 13). Perhaps one reason for his reluctance either to give up or radically change his painting was the modest but measurable success it had brought him. In the ten years since his marriage the family's finances had often been precarious, and once he had been threatened with the dreaded necessity of returning to commercial lithography. But at the last moment either he or his wife made a sale, and they were able not only to continue their independent work but even to move to a more comfortable apartment at 123 West Tenth Street, where they lived for some eighteen years. From 1915 to 1918 they had three exhibitions together at the Daniel Gallery, while Zorach also showed at the Whitney Studio Club and with the Independents from 1917 on. It took courage to abandon a field in which he had begun to make both a reputation and a living, but in the end he had no choice; he was impelled toward sculpture by an instinct too strong to resist. In 1922 he painted his last oil, and while he has worked in watercolor throughout his life, it was in that year that he committed himself to his new career.

Zorach's involvement with sculpture began largely by accident. In the summer of 1917 he had taken his family to a deserted house in New Hampshire, Echo Farm, lent them by Mrs. Henry Fitch Taylor. There, while working on a series of block prints, he became so interested in one butternut panel that he developed it into the carved relief, *Waterfall* (fig. 21), his first piece of sculpture except for a spirited canon which he had modeled at the age of six. The next summer Mrs. Taylor invited a potter named Applegate to New Hampshire. With his technical help and using his kiln, Zorach did several small terracottas, including one of his child, *First Steps*. But from the beginning he preferred to carve, and between 1917 and 1922 he produced some twelve pieces in wood, using at first only a jackknife and a few of the simplest tools. He had no formal training as a sculptor, either at this time or later, but what had started as an avocation soon began to absorb him more than his painting.

From the beginning, Zorach's sculpture was less self-consciously "modern" than his oils. The earliest pieces, done before 1922, have, to be sure, a certain stylized look, suggesting the influence of various primitive arts, from African to Romanesque. There is even a hint of our native folk sculpture—cigar store Indians and ship figureheads—in certain works such as his *Floating Figure* (fig. 45) with its sweeping, compressed lines, although Zorach himself disclaims a debt in this direction. "I owe most," he says, "to the great periods of primitive carving in the past—not to the moderns or to the classical Greeks, but to the Africans, the Persians, the Mesopotamians, the archaic Greeks and of course to the Egyptians." He also seems to have derived a strong sense of gesture and its sculptural uses from the work which he did during these years with the Provincetown Players, the Wharf Players and other little theatre groups. With them he served not only as scene painter, but also as producer, actor and dancer, and the dance especially became for him a serious interest.

As long as Zorach continued to paint his cubist pictures, his sculpture reflected, though to a lesser degree, his preoccupation with angular surface patterns and the primitive sources (chiefly African) on which cubism itself had drawn. But from the moment that he gave up working in oil, he seems to have turned his back also on any conscious concern with the modern movements. From 1922 on, his mature style as a sculptor emerged rapidly. The *Mother and Child* (fig. 25) of that year is apparently a transitional piece; in the mannered curve of the neck and the angular bend of the leg it harks back to some of Zorach's painted figures. But in the fullness of the volumes, the monumentality of the composition and in its frank expression of tenderness, it strikes a new note in his art. The *Two Children* (fig. 24) of the same year, more fluid in its motion, rounder in its forms and less hieratic in design, goes a step further. Only the rigidness of one arm and the rectangular opposition of full-face and profile hint remotely at his earlier work. In all important respects, this piece announces clearly the path Zorach was to follow for many years.

Zorach seems to have found his direction and the sculptural means to implement it almost by instinct. He was not, of course, unaware of what other sculptors were doing, both here and abroad. From the beginning he showed a natural antipathy for the Rodin tradition of impressionist modeling. Faced with an exhibition of Degas' sculpture in 1926, he wrote, "Compared with true sculpture they have no repose, no abstract value in design or form, elements very essential to all real sculpture. . . . Real sculpture is something monumental, something hewn from a solid mass, something with repose, with inner and outer form; with strength and power."[4] Equally illuminating is his admiration of Brancusi's work, "an expression of the spirit of beauty in the form—say of a human body—

5. MIRAGE—SHIPS AT NIGHT. 1919. Oil. 32 x 26. The Downtown
Gallery.

rather than an expression of the appreciation of the human body itself as in the sculpture of Maillol. . . . Brancusi may reduce form to a spheroid, but never does he reduce it to emptiness. No matter how intense the simplification, it is always full and alive." Yet in all honesty he could not help adding, "The sleekness, the perfection, the nicety becomes as over-whelming as a mid-Victorian atmosphere. The eye craves for relief in surfaces."[5]

Like Brancusi, Zorach allied himself naturally with the growing number of modern sculptors who believed in the esthetic necessity of carving their own designs directly in the block of stone or wood rather than modeling them in clay to be copied by professional cutters in the harder material. Indeed Zorach was one of the first exponents of direct carving in this country, just as one might say—with a good deal of exaggeration—that he is now one of the last. From the beginning he found a deep satisfaction in the slow and patient process of freeing the image from its imprisoning block, watching the forms emerge and appear, paradoxically, to swell in volume as the block itself diminished. "The actual resistance of tough material is a wonderful guide," he said in a lecture on direct sculpture in 1930. "He [the sculptor] cannot make changes easily, there is no putting back tomorrow what was cut away today. His senses are constantly alert. . . . If something goes wrong there is the struggle to right the rhythm. And slowly the vision grows as the work progresses."

He also found, like other direct carvers, that the material itself had a constantly modifying effect on the artist's vision. The grain of the wood, the markings in the stone, the shape of the log or boulder all set limits and suggested possibilities. The curve of his *Floating Figure* (fig. 45) and the essential outlines of his *Reclining Cat* (fig. 43), hewn from a Maine boulder, were both determined to a large extent by the materials selected. Watching his daughter's rabbits one day, he realized that the stone which held their pen door shut was not unlike a crouching rabbit itself, and carved it into one. At all times in his career he has been sensitive to the characteristic qualities of his materials and has occasionally let them play a major role in determining his forms. In works such as these, the feel of the original material is preserved in the finished piece and is often heightened by leaving parts of the original surface untouched and other areas roughly marked by the sculptor's tools. The result is compactness, strength and the vivid sense of a sculptured object. "The most beautiful carvings are the most simple, where the stone is held in one complete mass, designed without projections."[6]

But Zorach also discovered early in his career that this aspect of direct carving, if pushed to its extreme, created limits too stringent to encompass his sculptural interests. He was seldom content to leave his

6. SISTERS. 1920. Oil. 40 x 26. The Downtown Gallery.

20

7. YOSEMITE FALLS. 1920.
Oil. 72 x 30. The Downtown
Gallery.

visions half imprisoned in the rock; he wanted them to emerge boldly and sing. "Art," he thought, "is the eternal realization of life," and life to him was the love of man and woman, the joyousness of childhood, the nearly painful beauty of all living things. Art without these was nothing, yet art must be more than these. "I may make a perfect copy of a figure and no matter how beautiful that figure, it would be the farthest thing from a work of art. . . . Art has the quality of being removed from the temporary; there is a radiance of the eternal about it."[7]

The answer, as it emerged in his work during the 1920's, was a sculpture of ample forms and rhythms which seem to grow out of the forms and rhythms of nature and yet which are simplified, generalized and concentrated into a sculptural monumentality. The simplifications are never as radical as those of Brancusi, for Zorach was by nature too deeply rooted in the concrete, but they are motivated by the same purpose —to distill the essential elements of life from his experience and to embody them in a truly sculptural form. Sculpture was thus both means and end; it was his expression of life's significance and of its own.

In 1923 Zorach began to work in stone and showed at once an affinity for the medium. *The Artist's Wife* (fig. 27), carved directly in a warm Tennessee marble in 1924, strikes that instinctive balance between a monumental simplicity and a remarkably subtle modeling of surfaces which was to remain a hallmark of Zorach's work hereafter. From this he progressed rapidly to more complex designs, as in his *Child with Cat* (fig. 28) of 1926 with its upward spiraling motion and its more varied play of textures. Impressive as these pieces are, they seem a meagre preparation for the work which immediately followed, the truly monumental *Mother and Child* (fig. 46) of 1927-30. It is extraordinary that this, unquestionably one of Zorach's finest sculptures and one of his most ambitious in conception and design, was produced so early in his career. It marked the quick end of his apprenticeship as a carver and his emergence as a leading figure in the field of American sculpture.

In preparation for the *Mother and Child*, Zorach modeled a small study in clay (fig. 47), which did little more than establish the rudiments of the design and from which he departed freely. Then for three years he carved on his three-ton block of Spanish Florida Rosa marble, patiently evolving the complicated rhythm of the forms. The work which emerged is different in many ways from his earlier pieces. While it strikes somewhat the same balance between simplification and subtlety of modeling, the larger scale permitted the use of more massive volumes without loss of surface variety, and the artist has even increased these in his exaggeration of the heaviness of hands, legs and back. The distortion, though not marked, contributes both to the monumentality of the piece and to its emotional content, the sense of a protecting and nourishing motherhood. But it is in the design of the whole that the work shows the greatest development from Zorach's previous groups, for here he has done away with the frontality which is so marked in *Pegasus* (fig. 29) or the *Mother and Child* (fig. 25) of 1922. The influence of the block itself has dwindled, and the composition is conceived completely in the round. The interlocking of the figures, the flowing progression of the main forms and of the spaces between them, the relaxed turn of heads and bodies all lead the eye around the piece, up and down, forward and backward with a slow and fugue-like rhythm. In its clarity, its unbroken contours, its balance and its harmonious structure, it is a truly classical work of art, and one of the few which our predominantly romantic age has produced.

During the same years that Zorach was transforming himself from a painter to a sculptor, his life began to settle into a pattern which reflected both his character and his needs as an artist. It has altered little since. The country has always drawn him powerfully. "The wonder of life and nature is ever present," he once wrote on a scrap of paper. "In the growth of every blade of grass and flower, every child and animal, every breeze and storm is the significance of the greater mystery around and about us." From the time of his marriage he had taken his family every summer to the country: to New Hampshire, to Maine, Cape Cod and California. About 1923 they discovered and bought an old farm on the edge of the sea at Robinhood, Maine, and nearly half of their life has been spent there since. Many of the animals that Zorach has carved and many of the stones in which he has carved them are the animals and stones of Robinhood Farm. The cycle of the seasons, the work in the fields, his children's play and the joy of carving under the Maine sky have entered deeply into his work and more than once have inspired him to poetic utterance.

> "I have lifted great rocks for forty years
> And piled them up around the fields.
> In the evening I watch the sun go down behind the mountain;
> Straight lines of sky cross my eyes.
> I become light and delicate as the kitten sitting on the window sill,
> I am vapor,
> Or am I part of the last soft glow of the sun on the tree trunks?"

But Zorach is a man of the city, too. He needs contact with his fellow artists and with the varied activities of New York. He is a born teacher, as he discovered by accident when he met Caroline Pratt of the City and Country School on his trip to California in 1920. Out of this meeting grew an arrangement whereby Zorach gave art classes at the school in return for his daughter's tuition. Before long he found himself writing and lecturing on progressive methods of teaching art to children, and between 1920 and 1935 he gave courses in a number of other schools; the Walden School, the Birch Wathen School and Rosemary Hall in Greenwich, Connecticut. His longest teaching assignment, however, has been at the Art Students League where he has taught sculpture continuously

24

8. ROCKY CLIFFS—
YOSEMITE VALLEY. 1920.
Watercolor. 18½ x 13.
Collection of Mr. and Mrs.
Laurance S. Rockefeller.

from 1929 to the present. In addition, he has been a lecturer on the history of sculpture at Columbia University (1932-35) and has talked to countless groups from Skowhegan, Maine, to Austin, Texas, and from ladies' clubs to university audiences. While Zorach's teaching started from necessity, aggravated by the difficulty of selling sculpture during the long depression of the 1930's, it has continued long beyond his period of financial need.

For a living sculptor, Zorach has been remarkably successful. In 1924 he had his first one-man exhibition of sculpture (it also included water-colors and some of his earlier oils) at the Kraushaar Galleries. After one more show there, in 1928, he moved to the Downtown Gallery, which has handled his work ever since. His exhibition at the latter in 1931 was an important milestone in the growth of his reputation. It included only

9. YOSEMITE FALLS, I. 1920.
Watercolor. 14¾ x 12½. Collection
of Mr. and Mrs. Laurance S.
Rockefeller.

eight carvings and one drawing, but among them was the sensitive
adolescent figure, *The Artist's Daughter* (fig. 30), almost Egyptian in
pose and simplicity but filled with an undefinable quality of revery, and,
in contrast, the sprightly *Bathing Girl* (fig. 34) of highly polished
mahogany. There was a cat, a torso, a head, a small seated figure, but
above all, and the center of the show, there was the monumental *Mother
and Child* (fig. 46) completed the preceding year. Zorach and a group of
his students had risen at five in the morning and had trundled it to the
gallery through the empty, pre-dawn streets. Before the year was out, it
had won him his first important award, the Art Institute of Chicago's
fifteen-hundred-dollar Logan prize for sculpture. It was in 1931, too, that
his first works entered a museum, the Whitney Museum of American Art
acquiring his *Pegasus* (fig. 29) and two smaller pieces.

A year later, in 1932, the first of many artistic controversies broke
around Zorach's head, distressing him greatly at the time but adding
eventually to his reputation. With two other sculptors, Robert Laurent
and Gwen Lux, he had been commissioned to do a figure symbolizing
the dance for Radio City Music Hall. Because of the nature of the com-

mission and the over-life-size figure he projected, Zorach gave up any idea of carving it and decided to model it in clay, to be cast in aluminum. Despite this radical change in process, his *Spirit of the Dance* (fig. 32) is close to his *Mother and Child* stylistically—a little more open in form and making more use of graceful gesture, but with the same classical simplicity, the same slow rhythms and ample volumes. When it was done he felt, with justice, that it ranked high among his major pieces, and he was completely unprepared for the reaction of S. L. Rothafel ("Roxy"), manager of the Music Hall, who declared it too nude for his public and refused to place it on exhibition. The fact that the same fate befell the works of Laurent and Lux did little to ease the blow, but in the end

10. YOSEMITE FALLS, II.
1920. Watercolor. 19¼ x 13.
Collection of Mr. and Mrs.
Laurance S. Rockefeller.

27

things turned out better than with many of his later commissions. Edith Halpert promptly placed the plaster version on exhibition at the Downtown Gallery, where it won highly favorable reviews. Nelson Rockefeller protested Roxy's action, as did Edwin Alden Jewell, art critic of the *New York Times*, and several artists' organizations. Finally all three pieces were restored to view in the Music Hall, though relegated to less prominent positions than originally planned.

Just a year after the *Spirit of the Dance*, Zorach did one more major work in clay, eventually to be cast in bronze. This was *The Embrace* (fig. 37), the frankest of several pieces which were to come dealing with the theme of physical love. The difference between *Embrace* and its more famous prototype by Rodin, *The Kiss,* reveals much of Zorach's attitude and character. Where Rodin held the two bodies apart, straining poignantly against the desire that draws them together, Zorach has united them with a nearly pagan unselfconsciousness which does much to obliterate the erotic content. If it is not one of his most successful works from a purely esthetic point of view (perhaps because of a certain straining toward heroic types and proportions), it is nevertheless a testament to his own uncomplicated acceptance of life on every level of experience.

Soon Zorach returned to carving, or rather he never gave it up. "To me direct sculpture is greater than modelled sculpture," he reaffirmed in 1935, "its problems are greater and its possibilities of creative expression are deeper."[8] He began to explore new materials and new approaches. Working in the extremely hard Labrador granite, he produced one of his most abstract and radically simplified pieces, the *Torso* (fig. 35) of 1932, which almost suggests Brancusi in the precise flow of its lines and volumes. Working in York fossil, a relatively soft marble, he experimented with an open composition (*Affection*, fig. 36) cutting complete voids between the figures of child and dog. On the whole, however, he continued to prefer a more massive and sculptural approach. The *Child on Pony* (fig. 39) of the following year, although carved in the same stone and offering the same opportunities for an open design, is held closer to the form of the block, with no pierced areas. And in many pieces, such as the charming small *Pigeon* (fig. 31), the *Reclining Cat* (fig. 43), the *Hound* (fig. 38) and the mahogany *Youth* (fig. 40) of 1935, he kept even closer to the original form of his log and boulders.

Zorach's development, though never departing far from the well-defined direction he has chosen, has nevertheless varied quite widely in style and technique. "I have no set rule of procedure in carving," he wrote in 1935. "Sometimes I let the stone suggest its possibilities. Sometimes I work from drawings. Sometimes I make a small rough model in clay . . . [which] will give a sense of dimension and depth, of direction and planes. . . . Cutting into the stone without a preliminary sketch . . . too often results in a four-sided silhouette or a rounded form too closely bound to the original mass of the stone."[9] As if to illustrate his diversity of approaches, Zorach worked simultaneously, between 1936 and 1939, on two pieces which are as far apart as any in his career. One, the *Tiger, Tiger* relief (fig. 55), was carved roughly from a thick oak plank with the marks of the chisel left on the surface to emphasize its hewn character. Stylistically it returns to the arbitrary proportions and schematic design of primitive art; it is vigorous and decorative in the best sense of the word. The other is one of his major works in stone, the marble group called *Youth* (fig. 49), which took him three years to complete. Here, in contrast, the figures have been freed entirely from the volume of the original rock and have been modeled and polished until their swelling forms seem more like flesh than stone. It is perhaps Zorach's most naturalistic carving (aside from certain commissions), and if it has lost some of his sculptural quality, there is no question but that it restates the theme of physical attraction with extraordinary vitality.

11. CALIFORNIA REDWOODS. 1920. Pencil. 13½ x 10¼ (overall). The Downtown Gallery.

Throughout these years—indeed through the major part of his career—Zorach has found relaxation, and something more too, in painting watercolors. "I must be a dual personality," he says. "I started as a painter, and psychologically a part of me still is one." His watercolors fill several needs which his sculpture cannot: they are an outlet for his love of color, they are a direct means of interpreting the moods of nature, and they have a free spontaneity which is at the opposite pole from the slow, patient process of carving. Every summer, and sometimes on winter vacations, Zorach paints a small group of them.

In his earliest papers, such as the Yosemite series of 1920, Zorach used a dry technique not unlike that of Marin or Demuth, but in nearly all his later work he has preferred to paint on a very wet paper, a process which imposes problems of control but which yields a greater depth and richness of color. He is a "pure" watercolorist, never using opaque pigment and delighting in the brilliance of transparent washes. Many of his paintings deal primarily with light, a concern reflected in such titles as *Morning Glow, Autumn* (fig. 19) or *Early Morning Light*. He is extremely skillful in handling not only the glitter of Maine sunlight on snow or water, but also the subtler effects of fog, of dusk, of early dawn. Despite the spontaneity of these papers and the evanescent effects they capture, they are far from casual in organization. Zorach's designs are generally simple and dictated by the mood and nature of his subjects, but they are firmly stated—the sweeping curves of *Popham Beach, No. 1, Maine* (fig. 17), the restless pattern of twisting strokes in *Windy Day—Lowe's Point* (fig. 18) or the solid verticals and horizontals of *Robinhood Marina* (fig. 20) and many other paintings. "I am interested in interpretations rather than naturalism," Zorach says, and while the balance seems, in this day of predominantly abstract and expressionist art, closer to the naturalistic side of the equation, there can be no doubt that these watercolors speak in form as well as in subject of the joy and the serenity their author finds in nature.

Zorach has needed this respite, for much of his later career has been fraught with the struggles, disappointments, defeats and partial victories attendant on a long series of public commissions which his growing fame has won him. Early in his career he had written prophetically, "The big possibilities in the decoration of our public buildings have fallen to organizations of professional and commercial shops. The artist is left in his studio to do fragments; a torso, a head, a small figure that he can carry around without difficulty and expense. He cannot prove that he can do other things without the opportunity to do them. You may say that is the artist's fault in not organizing himself on a basis with other business. At the same time the artist realizes too well that business ability in an artist is the wallop that sooner or later deals his art the death blow."[10] Too often this nearly happened in Zorach's own case; never the death blow, for in the final test he always stood firm against the commercial-

12. NEVADA FALLS,
YOSEMITE VALLEY. 1920.
Pencil. 18¾ x 11⅞.
The Downtown Gallery.

ization of his art, but there were compromises that he later regretted and there were heartbreaking losses of commissions after months of work because of compromises he would not make. Yet the dream—which is every sculptor's dream—persisted. Despite the fact that it has often proved itself a nightmare, it still persists.

In the beginning many of the commissions for which he tried were those offered in open competitions. The first of these, in 1932, was a Soviet-sponsored contest for a memorial to Lenin. Hopefully Zorach sent

off his plaster model to Moscow and waited. After months and a series of unanswered letters, he finally hired a lawyer who was able to discover only that it had been safely received. Two years later Zorach complained in a letter to the *New York Times* (March 8, 1934) that the Russians had stolen and mutilated his design for the monument which they had just erected in their capitol.

In spite of this inauspicious beginning, Zorach plunged into a veritable welter of competitions and commissions between 1935 and 1937, only one of which reached final fruition. He designed a colossal figure of Abraham Lincoln, still imposing in the photographs of the plaster sketch, which would have been twenty feet high if executed. This was for the New York debut of a play, which unfortunately never got beyond its tryout in Chicago. He then became involved in an incredibly complicated controversy over a memorial to Robert W. Speer, a former mayor of Denver, Colorado, which was to have been placed in that city's Civic Center. Two rival committees, each bitterly contesting the other's authority, picked different designs—one Zorach's, the other by a native Coloradan, Arnold Ronnebeck. The result was a heated deadlock, finally resolved by spending the money on a hospital instead.

Undaunted, Zorach entered an open competition for a *Memorial to the Pioneer Woman*, sponsored by the Texas Centennial Commission. To this he submitted the plaster model of a lyrical family group (fig. 44), the mother reading to her youngest child, father and son standing protectively behind her. Unhappily for the artist, they were nude, and when the professional jury appointed by the State Board of Control unanimously recommended Zorach's entry, the anguished protests from Texans swelled into a controversy dwarfing all previous ones. One astute observer noted that the woman wore no wedding ring, another quibbled that it was a memorial to a pioneer family, not to the pioneer woman as specified, while a chapter of the Daughters of the Republic of Texas declared it "the greatest insult that could be offered to these women who believed and practised the virtue of modesty."[11] In vain did Richard Foster Howard, then Director of the Dallas Museum of Fine Arts, come to Zorach's defense with public arguments on the esthetic merits of the work; in vain too did Zorach himself attempt to rescue the situation by constructing another model with lightly draped figures replacing the objectionable nudes. Texas was having none of this particular work of art.

The single exception in this series of misfortunes and misunderstandings was the over-life-size figure of Benjamin Franklin (fig. 41), carved in pink Tennessee marble, which Zorach completed in 1937 for the Benjamin Franklin Post Office in Washington, D.C. This had been commissioned some two years earlier by the Fine Arts Section of the U. S. Treasury Department as part of its intelligent program of obtaining the services of the country's best artists to adorn public buildings. Zorach gave many weeks of preparation to the project, studying the available likenesses of Franklin, the costume of the period and working at length on a pose which would express both the benevolence and majesty of the figure. And in spite of its naturalism and all the historically correct detailing of dress, the work does indeed have an imposing largeness of conception and a strength of characterization which make it not only one of Zorach's most successful commissions but also one of the best public monuments to an individual in America.

The year 1939 saw Zorach engaged in two more commissions, though only one of these was executed. With one hundred other artists, he entered the first stage of a competition for the Thomas Jefferson Memorial in Washington, but was passed over in favor of the predominantly academic group of sculptors selected to compete in the second stage. While he was later invited to enter the second stage (as an alternate to Maurice Sterne, who had withdrawn), his free interpretation of Jefferson—done perhaps in reaction to the painstaking research for his *Franklin*—failed to impress the jury. More successful in its outcome was the huge plaster group, *Builders of the Future* (fig. 48), which he executed for New York City's World's Fair in the same year. While it is in some respects Zorach's most conventional monument—perhaps because of the nature of the theme with which he had to cope—its sheer size, sixteen feet high, and its balanced pyramidal composition dominated the spacious setting.

For nearly ten years Zorach undertook no more major public commissions, and he has never again entered an open competition. During the last decade, however, he has been tempted by several opportunities to do monumental or architectural works, with results as mixed as those of his earlier essays. In 1949 he was one of several sculptors commissioned to submit designs for a memorial on Riverside Drive to the six million Jews who perished under Nazi persecution. Zorach's model (fig. 67) is built around an imposing monolith with the heroic figure of a Jewish man on one side, a mother and her child on the other. In its simplicity, its directness of statement and its depth of feeling it is one of his best works in this vein. The fact that it was not accepted is of only academic interest today, since the sponsoring committee ran into financial difficulties and the entire project was abandoned. In compensation, Zorach's next important commission, a big relief for the façade of the Mayo Clinic building in Rochester, Minnesota (figs. 73-4), was accomplished without harassments in two years (1952-53) and was put in place the following year. In this work, with its open design, the bronze figures are held out from the wall on steel rods and seem to float lightly in space, an impression heightened by their sweeping contours. While they illustrate an inspirational theme, man at work, Zorach has not permitted it to interfere with his essentially decorative concept. It is probably his most successful architectural adornment.

The story of Zorach's architectural work, up to the present moment, ends on a sadder note. Early in 1956 he had nearly completed a very large aluminum relief (figs. 83-4), commissioned by the Second National Bank of Houston, Texas. This was, by today's standard, relatively conservative in style—perhaps even more so than his work for the Mayo Clinic. The symbolic figures are more naturalistic and they are grouped in more statically balanced compositions. A series of preliminary models had been submitted and approved by the bank and for months the artist had been working on the full-scale model and supervising the casting, section by section, of the finished relief.

This was the situation in January, 1956, when Zorach became involved, through no fault of his own, in one of the political controversies which swept the art world in those hysterical days. An exhibition, Sport in Art, sponsored by the magazine *Sports Illustrated* and assembled by the American Federation of Arts, had been quietly touring the country

14. SEATED NUDE. 1942. Pencil. 18½ x 22. The Downtown Gallery.

and was about to have a scheduled showing at the Dallas Museum of Fine Arts. On January 12 the Dallas County Patriotic Council requested the museum to remove from the show works by four artists, including Zorach (who was represented by a watercolor of an elderly fisherman) on the ground that their authors had Communist or Communist-front records. The fact that the museum rejected the demands of its self-appointed censors, that the Federation reaffirmed its strong policy of artistic freedom, that Zorach hotly denied Communist leanings of any kind and was vouched for by his Maine representative in Congress did not obscure the unpleasant publicity.

15. TWO FIGURES. 1929. Crayon and pencil. 29¼ x 20. The Downtown Gallery.

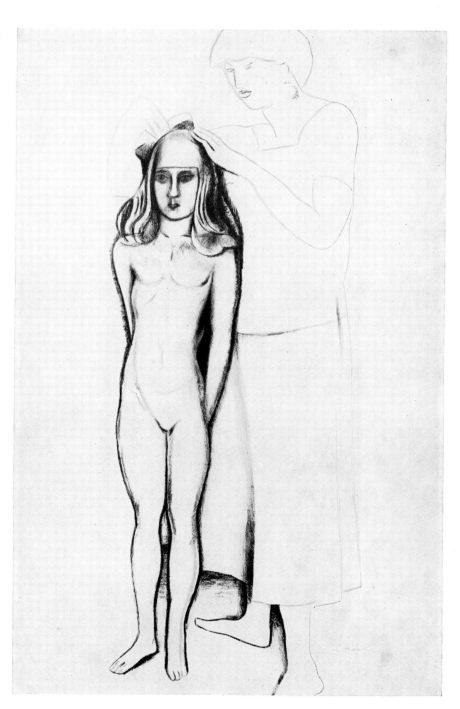

16. DAHLOV. 1935. Ink.
23⅜ x 18⅜ (overall). The
Downtown Gallery.

On February 14 the bank notified Zorach that it would not accept
or place on its building his relief, then about eighty per cent completed.
The decision was totally unexpected, since the bank had been paying for
the casting as it progressed and had shown no evidence of discontent
with the designs. Its explanations varied but made very little sense. At
one point it said the relief had been rejected because the bank had recently
changed its name to Bank of the Southwest, but since the relief was a
symbolic representation of Texas history, it would appear to have been
more rather than less appropriate. At another point it declared the work
too modern for its new aluminum and granite structure, but at the same
time it commissioned Rufino Tamayo to paint a nearly abstract mural
for its interior. While Zorach finally won a financial settlement which
permitted him to complete the casting, and while plans have finally been
made for the erection of the relief on a new university building in the
East, the experience was a heartbreaking one that affected him profoundly.

In spite of this experience and the many other disappointments which have attended his public commissions, Zorach has never relinquished his dream of creating monumental sculpture for permanent settings. Over and over he has resolved not to be drawn again into the battles with architects, the fickle decisions of committees and the compromises demanded by a client's dubious taste, but when an opportunity presents itself he can seldom refuse. Today he is working on the model of a big limestone relief for New York's Municipal Court Building on Center Street. It may not be one of his greatest works—it is doubtful if any of his public commissions is—but it will have a truly sculptural quality vastly superior to the conventional academic decorations which grace so many of our buildings. Indeed Zorach has probably done more than any other living American artist to break the hold of what he called, back in 1930, the "professional and commercial shops" on work of this kind.

Since 1940, Zorach's more intimate sculpture has developed along three fairly distinct lines, which might be called classical, primitive and romantic, although all are informed by his individual style and share other common characteristics inherent in the process of direct carving. Of these directions, the classical, growing out of such earlier pieces as the big *Mother and Child* (fig. 46) and *Spirit of the Dance* (fig. 32), has been dominant. Three major works in this vein are *The Future Generation* (fig. 64), *Devotion* (fig. 56) and *The Family* (fig. 86), in all of which he has explored further the theme of maternity, emphasizing to an even greater degree than before the ample, swelling volumes of his figures. While they are completely released from the original block of stone, echoes of its shape and solidity are sensed in the designs—rectangular in the first, cylindrical in the last two. "A piece of sculpture is made up of silhouettes," Zorach wrote at about this time, "which move in a spiral, which must function at every angle of the sphere. I like to be able to roll a stone piece around on the ground so that I can look at it from every position. You cannot do this with a model of clay."[12] The feeling of a free and rhythmical movement following the boundaries of the original stone is strong in all these pieces. There is also an interior organization of marked clarity, each part distinct—an arm, a leg, a head— yet each related to the whole with a kind of architectural logic. The result is a serenity, a poise and an emotional restraint which encompasses the tenderness of the theme but holds it within purely sculptural bounds.

The same innate classicism informs many of Zorach's single figures and heads, one of the most impressive examples being his majestic *Victory* (fig. 63) of 1945. In this, even more than in the groups, a continuous silhouette, changing but meaningful from every angle, bounds the piece with a flowing contour of great vitality. It marks Zorach's closest approach to Greek sculpture and might well be described by his own words on archaic Greek art in one of his Columbia lectures: "the direct simplicity, the decorative treatment and purity of form without fears, complexes and inhibitions, but with a simple pure loveliness." His work in this vein is not neo-classical; it is a modern reaffirmation of the classical spirit, the classical virtues, the classical sense of harmony and form. It grows from his own nature and illuminates the majority of his work, expressing itself in the massive repose of *The Faith of This Nation* (fig. 53), the decorative arabesque of *Awakening* (fig. 54), the poised action of *Puma* (fig. 78) and the monumental quality (more truly so than in his actual monuments) of a whole series of heads from the *Christ* (fig. 52) of 1940 to the porphyry *Woman* (fig. 88) of 1958.

Yet Zorach has not always been content to stay within classical disciplines. Something in his character has always responded to the beauty and authority of arts still more primitive than the archaic Greek—those tribal and religious images which are not symbols or interpretations, but pure magic. In a number of small works such as the mask-like *Head* (fig. 69) of 1952, the pink granite *Head* (fig. 81) of 1954, or his *John the Baptist* (fig. 82) of the same year, Zorach has used the universal primitive conventions of staring eyes and heavily carved eyelids, together with a

17. POPHAM BEACH, NUMBER 1, MAINE. c. 1940. Watercolor. 15 x 22. The Downtown Gallery.

variety of radical simplifications and departures from naturalism to create strangely totemic effects. At other times he has diverged from his classicism in a more romantic direction, which has approached expressionism in the nature of its distortions. His *Man of Judah* (fig. 70) with its compressed and elongated features was perhaps his first step in this direction, carried still further in the oddly asymmetrical and brooding *Head* (fig. 76) of 1954. The most impressive example, however, and certainly the most extreme, is his rugged *Head of Moses* (fig. 85) of 1956, hewn from a block of granite with a violence of form and of feeling quite unlike anything Zorach had done before. The tortured features, the heavily exaggerated planes, the deep undercutting which creates an irregular pattern of light and shadow, all contribute to the unrestrained emotional impact of the piece. Though far from the line of his main direction, it is one of his most powerful works.

In 1932 Zorach took part in a debate at the Whitney Museum on the subject, "Nationalism in Art—Is it an Advantage?" Speaking, with

18. WINDY DAY—LOWE'S POINT. c. 1950. Watercolor. 15 x 22. Collection of Mr. and Mrs. Laurance S. Rockefeller.

19. MORNING GLOW, AUTUMN. 1958. Watercolor. 13⅜ x 20. The
Downtown Gallery.

Richard Lahey, for the affirmative (against Maurice Sterne and Joseph
Pollet for the negative), Zorach said in part: "When I speak of national
art I do not mean the superficial concern with immediate surroundings.
Painting Jewish types does not create a Jewish art, nor concentration on
the American scene make an American artist. The artist himself should
not be concerned with whether or not he is creating American art, but if
his roots are firmly planted in the soil, its flavor will permeate his work
no matter what subject or forms he uses."[13]

Transplanted from Lithuania to the rocky coast of Maine, Zorach's
own roots have grown with something of this simple inevitability. His
sculpture is not topically American. It deals with the universal themes
of man and woman, maternity, children and animals. But it has also a
spaciousness, a freedom and an untrammeled joy in living, which are
perhaps the reflection of the artist's natural development in a corner of
the world that has given him, along with its hardships, an abundance of
these same qualities.

He has repaid his debt by playing a major role—together with Gaston
Lachaise, Robert Laurent, Elie Nadelman and, at the most, one or two

others—in rescuing American sculpture from the neo-classical inanities and illustrative modeling which dominated it at the turn of the century. From the early 'teens to about 1930 this small group formed an isolated avant garde in our country. And of them all, Zorach probably did the most to establish here the practice of direct carving and the esthetic concepts which grew out of it, just as he has had the greatest influence, by teaching and example, on a following generation.

Today, the school that Zorach did so much to found has become the conservative one. A younger group has rebelled, in its turn, against the limitations of carving and has endowed sculpture with a wider range of expression by building it out of metal with the welding torch, piercing it, projecting it, admitting light and space to its very core and turning it toward a more abstract imagery. Fruitful as this has been, it is a basically different concept of the art, closer to painting in the freedom of its means, and it has inevitably sacrificed many of the carver's goals: the compact-

20. ROBINHOOD MARINA. 1958. Watercolor. 21½ x 28½. The Downtown Gallery.

ness, the intrinsic beauty of materials, the sensuous tactile values, the subtlety of modeling, the variety of surface and the concrete imagery. As long as these qualities are prized, it seems likely that the work of the traditional carvers will continue to play a part in American sculpture.

Zorach, for one, is unwilling to abandon them. Not only are they essential to his conscious esthetic credo; they have become an almost instinctive part of his whole creative process. The technical limitations of carving are, to him, its strength. The only tragic limitation would be to work by formula, without feeling. "The quality of art is feeling," he wrote recently, "to feel so deeply that you inject that power into your own work and convey it to others."[14] Though his subjects change little, they move him today as deeply as in youth. Though his materials are the same, they still suggest endlessly new possibilities. At seventy-two Zorach is carving wood and stone, as he has for forty-two years, in the image of his own largeness of spirit, his own serene response to life.

NOTES: Quotations from published sources are identified by reference to the Bibliography. All other quotations are from mss., letters or conversations with the artist, unless otherwise noted.

1. Bibl. 8.
2. Bibl. 3.
3. Bibl. 8.
4. Bibl. 13.
5. Bibl. 12.
6. Bibl. 15.
7. Bibl. 16.
8. Bibl. 15.
9. Bibl. 15.
10. Bibl. 16.
11. Bibl. 116.
12. Bibl. 20a.
13. Bibl. 7.
14. Bibl. 9.

Plates

21. WATERFALL. 1917. Butternut
wood. 14 high. Collection of
Mrs. Samuel Wolman.

22. KIDDIE CAR. 1920. Rosewood. 19 high.
The Downtown Gallery.

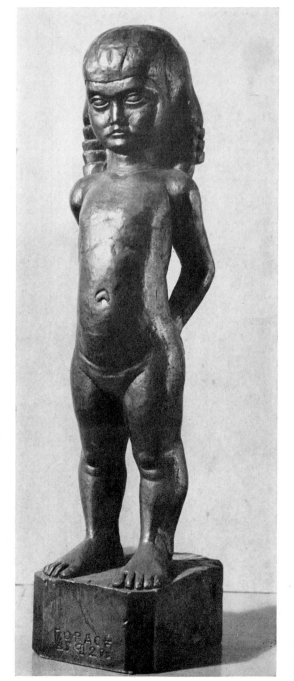

23. FIGURE OF A CHILD. 1921. Mahogany.
23 high. Collection of Dr. Edward J. Kempf.

24. TWO CHILDREN. 1922. Mahogany. c. 36 high. Collection of Theodore Frost.

25. MOTHER AND
CHILD. 1922. Mahogany.
36 high. Collection of Mr.
and Mrs. Lathrop Brown.

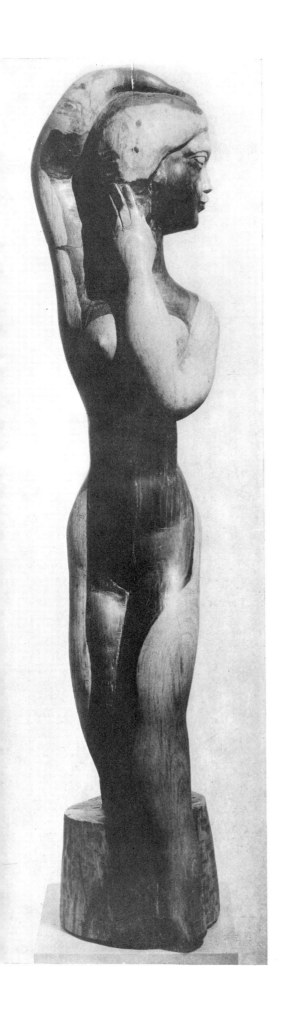

26. FIGURE OF A GIRL. 1923. Lignum vitae.
    48 high. Owner unknown.

27. THE ARTIST'S WIFE. 1924. Tennessee
    marble. 18 high. The Downtown Gallery.

28. CHILD WITH CAT. 1926. Tennessee marble. 18 high.
Museum of Modern Art, New York. Gift of Mr. and Mrs.
Sam A. Lewisohn.

29. PEGASUS. 1925. Walnut. 15 high. Whitney Museum of
American Art, gift of Mrs. Juliana Force.

30. THE ARTIST'S DAUGHTER.
1930/1946. Replica of damaged original
done in 1930. Georgia marble. 25½ high.
Whitney Museum of American Art.

31. PIGEON. c. 1930. Labrador marble.
9½ long. Collection of Mr. and Mrs.
Laurance S. Rockefeller

32. SPIRIT OF THE DANCE. 1932. Plaster model for aluminum casting. 78 high.
Radio City Music Hall.

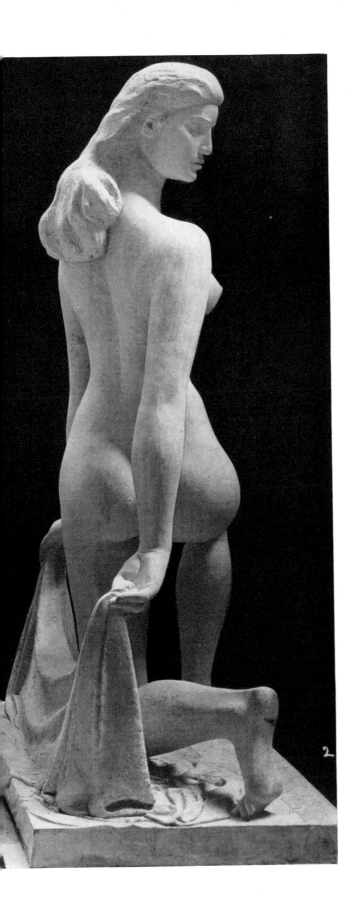

33. HILDA. 1932. Egyptian marble. 13 high.
Cone Collection, Baltimore Museum of Art.

34. BATHING GIRL. 1930. Borneo
mahogany. 48 high. Norma and John
Marin, Jr., Collection.

35. TORSO. 1932. Labrador granite. 33 high. Sara Roby Foundation.

37. THE EMBRACE. 1933. Bronze. 66 high. The Downtown Gallery.

36. AFFECTION. 1933. York fossil marble. 31½ high. Munson-Williams-Proctor Institute.

38. HOUND. 1935. Granite boulder. 24 long.
The Downtown Gallery.

39. CHILD ON PONY. 1934. York fossil marble.
25 high. The Downtown Gallery.

40. YOUTH. 1935. Borneo mahogany. 51 high.
The Downtown Gallery.

41. BENJAMIN FRANKLIN. 1936-37.
Pink Tennessee marble. 90 high. Benjamin
Franklin Post Office, Washington, D. C.

42. SEATED CAT. 1937. Swedish granite.
17¾ high. The Metropolitan Museum of
Art, Purchase, Edward C. Moore, Jr.,
Gift Fund, 1937.

43. RECLINING CAT. 1935. Granite. 17
long. The Downtown Gallery.

44. MEMORIAL TO THE PIONEER WOMAN. 1936. Plaster
model.

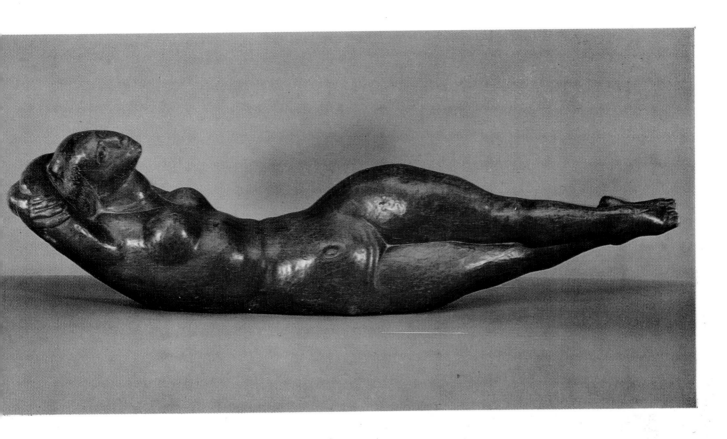

45. FLOATING FIGURE. 1922. African mahogany. 33¼ long. Room of Contemporary
Art Collection, Albright Art Gallery, Buffalo, N. Y.

46. MOTHER AND CHILD. 1927-30. Spanish Florida Rosa marble. 65˝
high. The Metropolitan Museum of Art, Fletcher Fund, 1952.

46. MOTHER AND CHILD. 1927-30. Spanish Florida Rosa marble. 65
high. The Metropolitan Museum of Art, Fletcher Fund, 1952.

47. MOTHER AND CHILD. 1927-30. Clay model (c. 16 high) and stages in carving.

48. BUILDERS OF THE
FUTURE. 1939. Plaster.
c. 16 feet high. New York
World's Fair.

49. YOUTH. 1936-39. Botticini marble. 47 long. Norton Gallery and School of Art.

50. QUEST. 1942-43. Pentelic marble. 23 high. The Roland P. Murdock Collection, Wichita Art Museum.

51. NIMBUS. 1941. Pink granite. 12 high. The Downtown Gallery.

52. HEAD OF CHRIST. 1940. Black granite. 15 high. Museum of Modern Art. Mrs. John D. Rockefeller, Jr., Fund.

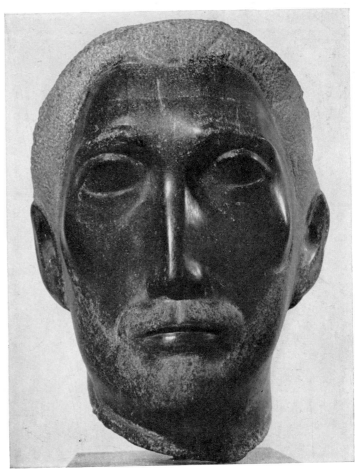

53. FAITH OF THIS NATION. 1939-42. Georgia white marble. 28 long. Collection of Wright Ludington.

54. AWAKENING. 1942. Colorado alabaster. 34 long. Virginia Museum of Fine Arts, Richmond.

55. TIGER, TIGER. 1943. Oak. 39 long. The Downtown Gallery.

56. DEVOTION. 1946. Granite. 34 high. Collection of Mr. and Mrs. Laurance S. Rockefeller.

57. HEAD OF A PROPHET.
1946. Black granite. 16½ high.
The Art Institute of Chicago,
Harriott A. Fox Fund.

58. HEN. c. 1946. 16 long.
Collection of J. H. Hirshhorn.

59. TREE INTO WOMAN.
1945. Rosewood. 55 high.
The Downtown Gallery.

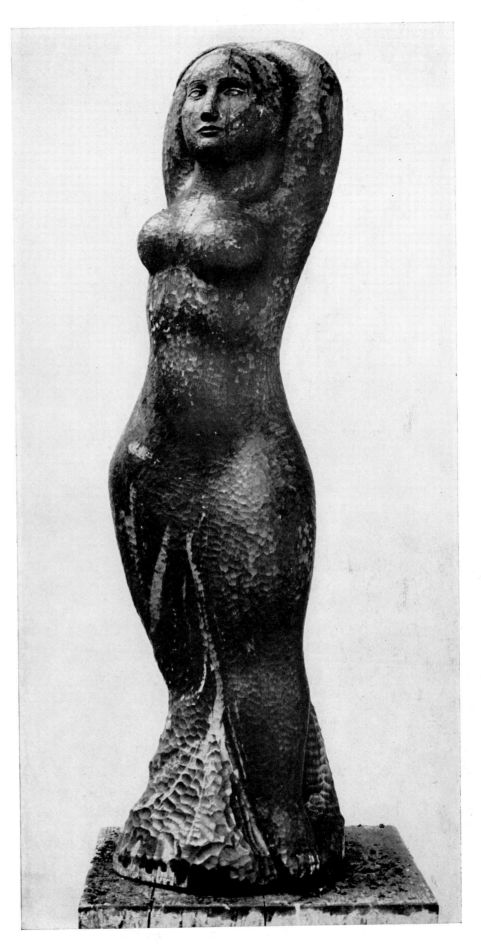

60. SERENITY. 1947.
    Granite boulder. 12½ high.
    Collection of Jack Lawrence.

61. ADAM. c. 1948.
    Granite boulder. 11½ high.
    F. M. Hall Collection,
    University of Nebraska.

62. MASK. 1946. Onyx. 10 high. Collection of Mr. and Mrs. John J. Carney.

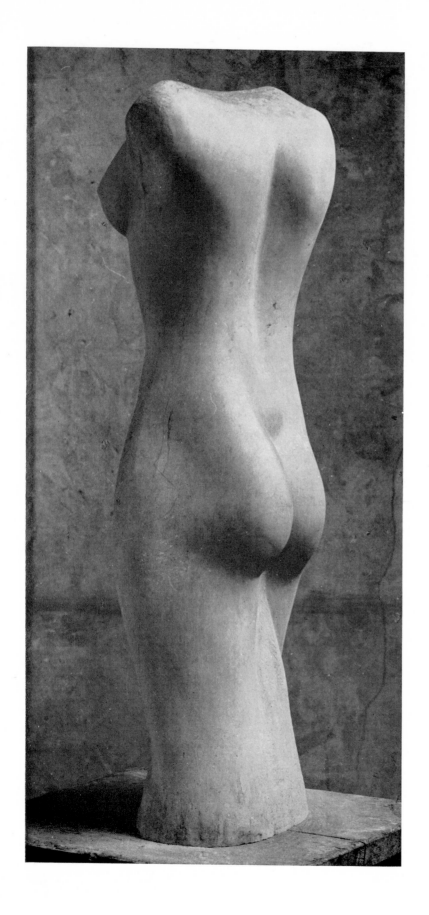

63. VICTORY. 1945. French marble. 43 high.
   The Downtown Gallery.

64. THE FUTURE GENERATION. 1942-47. Botticini marble. 40 high.
Whitney Museum of American Art.

65. THE GRAY RABBIT. 1947. Maine glacial boulder. 15 long. The Downtown Gallery.

66. HEAD OF YOUNG WOMAN. 1947. Pentelic marble.
21 high. The Downtown Gallery.

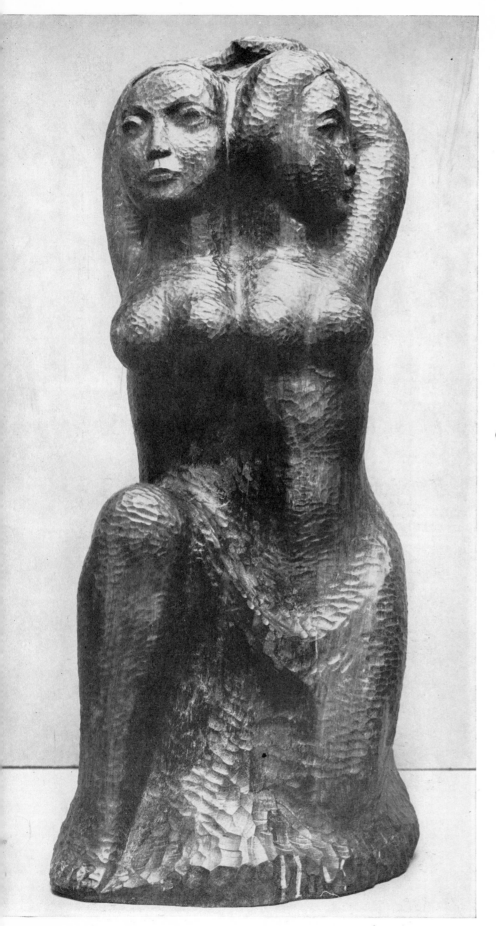

68. GEMINI. 1950. Wood. 32 high.
The Sonia and Michael Watter
Collection.

69. HEAD. 1952. Granite. 8¼ high.
    Collection of Mary and Sylvan Lang.

70. MAN OF JUDAH. 1950. Granite.
    17 high. The Downtown Gallery.

71. NEW HORIZON. 1951. Plaster model. 44 high.
The Downtown Gallery.

72. EVE. 1951. Granite. 26 high. Collection of J. H. Hirshhorn.

73. MAN AND WORK. (Mayo Clinic Relief,
    Rochester, Minnesota.) 1952-53. Clay model.

74. THE PURVEYORS. (Full-scale clay model for Mayo Clinic relief.) 6 feet long.

75. RECLINING FIGURE. 1954. Sienna marble. 17½ long. The Downtown Gallery.

76. HEAD. 1954. Onyx. 7½ high.
   Collection of Mr. and Mrs. Allan D. Emil.

77. HEAD OF MARATHONIAN. 1954.
   Green Porphyry. 11 high.
   The Downtown Gallery.

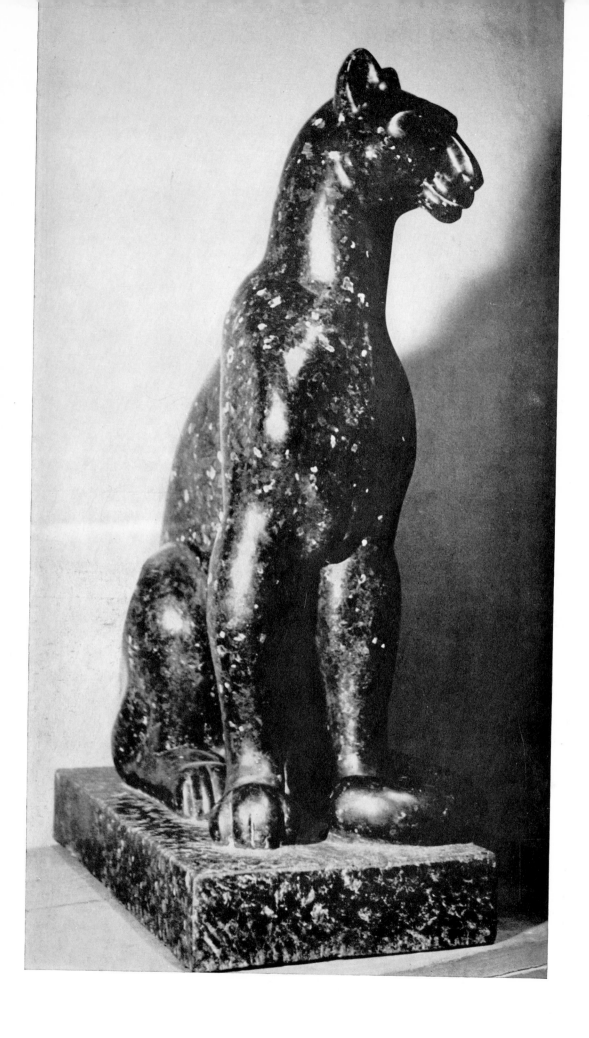

78. PUMA. 1954. Labrador granite. 40 high.
   The Downtown Gallery.

79. FROG. 1954. Green Maine granite. 10 high.
   The Downtown Gallery.

80. THE SEA GULL. 1954. Milan Italian marble.
   19½ long. The Downtown Gallery.

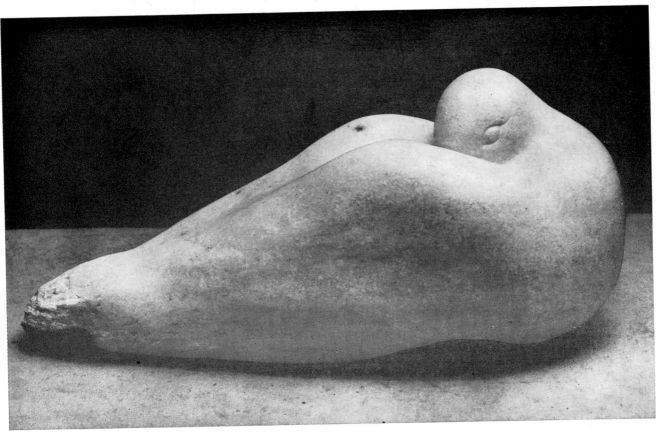

81. HEAD. 1954. Pink granite. 10½ high. The Downtown Gallery.

82. JOHN THE BAPTIST. 1955. Porphyry. 12 high. The Downtown Gallery.

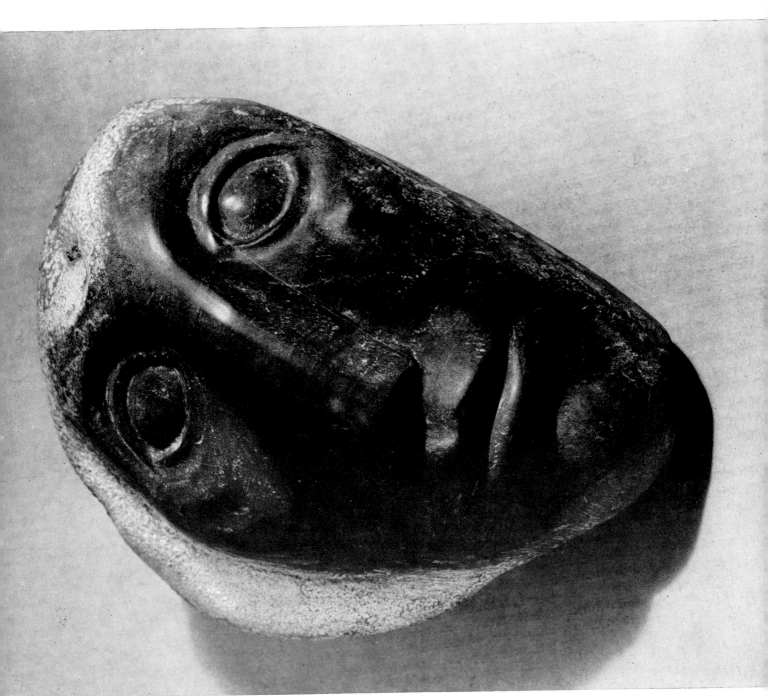

83. HEAD AND TORSO. (Full-scale clay models for *The New State of Texas*.) 1955.

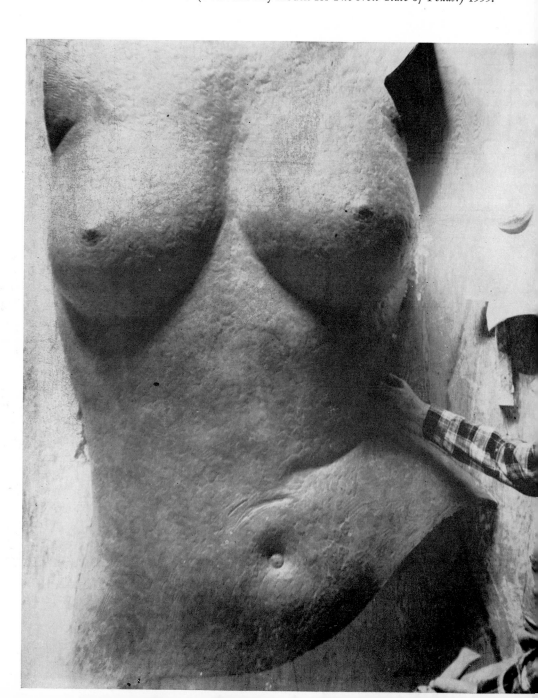

84. THE NEW STATE OF TEXAS.
(Originally commissioned by Second National
Bank, now Bank of the Southwest,
Houston, Texas.) 1955. Clay model.

85. HEAD OF MOSES. 1956. Granite. 36 high. Columbia University.

86. THE FAMILY. 1957. Granite. 20 high.
Collection of L. Arnold Weissberger.

87. YOUNG WOMAN. 1956. Pink
Milan marble. 21 high. Collection of
Mr. and Mrs. Arthur Miller.

88. WOMAN. 1958. Porphyry. 21½ high. The Downtown Gallery.

89. HEAD OF MICHELANGELO. 1957. Porphyry. 14½ high. Syracuse University.

90. LOVERS. 1958. Italian marble. 10¾ long. Collection of Miss Marilyn Karnes.

Chronology

1887   Born February 28, Eurburg, Lithuania, son of Orchick and Toba Bloch.

1891   To America with his mother and other children to join his father in Port Clinton, Ohio.

1894   To Cleveland, Ohio, with his family. Entered public school.

1900   Left school to work at various factory jobs, but returned to school after a year.

1902   Graduated from grammar school; took job as errand boy with Morgan Lithograph Company.

1903-1906   Apprenticed to same firm to learn lithography. Studied nights at Cleveland School of Art.

1907-1909   Winters in New York studying at National Academy of Design with A. M. Ward, George Maynard and others and about a month with George Bridgman at Art Students League. Summers in Cleveland working for Otis Lithograph Company.

1910-1911   In France, studying chiefly at La Palette with Jacques Emil Blanche and John Duncan Fergusson. Second summer sketching near Avignon, followed by brief trip to Switzerland and Germany. Paintings exhibited at Salon d'Automne, 1911.

1911-1912   In Cleveland working for Otis Lithograph Company; first one-man exhibition of paintings at Taylor Galleries. To New York in December, 1912, where he has lived since. Married Marguerite Thompson.

1913   Exhibited in Armory Show and at MacDowell Club.

1915   Son, Tessim, born.

1916   Showed work with other young modernists in Forum Exhibition. Summer, produced and acted in a play with the Provincetown Players. Continued to work with them in New York to 1918.

1917   Daughter, Dahlov, born. Summer at Echo Farm near Plainfield, New Hampshire, where he did his first wood carving.

1918   Summer in Plainfield, New Hampshire.

1919   Summer in Stonington, Maine.

1920   Summer in California, painting in Yosemite Park. Began teaching children at City and Country School (continued at Walden School, Birch Wathen School and Rosemary Hall to 1935).

1921   Returned to Provincetown for summer (also in 1922, 1923). Exhibited in Later Tendencies in Art exhibition at Pennsylvania Academy of the Fine Arts.

1922   Gave up painting for sculpture.

1924   Began spending summers on old farm at Robinhood, Maine, purchased the year before. Has summered there ever since. First one-man exhibition of his sculpture at Kraushaar Galleries.

1929   Began teaching sculpture at Art Students League, where he has continued to the present time.

1931   One-man exhibition at Downtown Gallery did much to establish his reputation. *Mother and Child* awarded Logan Prize at Art Institute of Chicago. Whitney Museum acquired three sculptures, his first to enter a public gallery.

1932   *Spirit of the Dance,* commissioned for Radio City Music Hall, rejected by "Roxy" as too nude, but eventually installed. Won Logan Prize for watercolor at Art Institute of Chicago.

1932-1935   Lecturer on sculpture at Columbia University.

1936   Won two important competitions, *Memorial to the Pioneer Woman* in Texas and *Memorial to Robert W. Speer* in Denver, but both became involved in controversies and were not erected. At about this time bought and remodelled old carriage house at 276 Hicks Street, Brooklyn, which has been his New York home and studio since.

1937   First public commission erected: *Benjamin Franklin* in Benjamin Franklin Post Office, Washington, D.C. Active in founding the Sculptors Guild.

1939   *Builders of the Future,* sixteen-foot high plaster group, installed at New York World's Fair.

1953   Elected to National Institute of Arts and Letters.

1954   Mayo Clinic reliefs installed on new building at Rochester, Minnesota.

1956   January, Dallas County Patriotic Council attacked Zorach as Communist sympathizer, demanded Dallas Museum withdraw his watercolor of fisherman from Sport in Art exhibition. Zorach denied charges and museum refused. February, Bank of the Southwest, Houston, Texas, cancelled commission for 30 x 32-foot aluminum relief which Zorach had nearly completed. May, Marion Koogler McNay Art Institute, San Antonio, Texas, held large exhibition of Zorach's sculpture in face of protests by American Legion.

1958   Commissioned by City of New York to design eighteen-foot limestone relief for Municipal Court Building on Center Street.

ONE-MAN EXHIBITIONS:

Taylor Galleries, Cleveland, 1912; Daniel Gallery, N. Y. (with Marguerite Zorach), 1915, 1916, 1918; O'Brien's Gallery, Chicago (with Marguerite Zorach), 1916; Studio of William and Marguerite Zorach, N. Y., 1919; Dayton Museum of Fine Arts (with Marguerite Zorach), 1922; Rochester Memorial Art Gallery, 1924; C. W. Kraushaar Art Galleries, N. Y., 1924, 1928; Arts and Crafts Club, New Orleans (with Marguerite Zorach), 1927; Downtown Gallery, N. Y., 1931, 1932, 1936, 1943, 1944, 1947, 1948, 1951, 1956; Ansel Adams Galleries, San Francisco, 1933; Philadelphia Art Alliance (with Marguerite Zorach), 1939; Rochester Memorial Art Gallery, 1941; California Palace of the Legion of Honor, San Francisco (with Marguerite Zorach), 1946; State Teachers College, New Paltz, N. Y., 1950; Art Students League, N. Y. (retrospective), 1950; Florida Gulf Coast Art Center, Belleair, 1952; Des Moines Art Center, 1954; Marion Koogler McNay Art Institute, San Antonio, 1956.

Selected Bibliography

The place of publication of books is New York unless otherwise noted.

ABBREVIATIONS: Ag August, Am American, Ap April, bibl bibliography, bul bulletin, D December, ed edited, F February, il illustration(s), Ja January, Je June, Jl July, mag magazine, Mr March, My May, N November, O October, p page(s), pl plates, S September, sup supplement.

WRITINGS BY ZORACH

1. American Sculpture. *Studio* 127:185-7 Je 1944. 6 il.

2. The Artist's Point of View. *New York City Art Center Bul* 8:126-7 Je 1930.

3. The Background of an Artist. Part I: Early Years. *Mag of Art* 34:162-8 Ap 1941. 8 il.; Part II: Productive Years 34:234-9 My 1941. 7 il.

4. The Child and Art. *Arts* 16:394-7 F 1930. 3 il.

5. Explanatory Note. *The Forum Exhibition of Modern American Painters*, 1916. 1 il.

6. [Foreword.] *William Zorach*, 1945. bibl 41.

7. Nationalism in Art—Is It an Advantage? [In "The Debate."] *Art Digest* 6:15,21-2 Mr 15 1932.

8. The New Tendencies in Art. *Arts* 2:10-15 O 1921.

9. The Nude in Photography and Art. *Esquire* 38:77-83 O 1952. 12 il.

10. Rhythm in Sculpture. *Am Artist* 13:34-6 F 1949. 5 il. Reprinted from bibl 18, chapter 6.

11. Sculpture at the Fair. *Mag of Art* 30:39 Ja 1937.

12. The Sculpture of Constantin Brancusi. *Arts* 9:143-50 Mr 1926. 9 il.

13. The Sculpture of Edgar Degas. Arts 8:263-5 N 1925. 2 il.

14. [Statement.] Newark Museum: *American Paintings and Sculpture from the Museum's Collections*, 1944, p 170. 1 il.

15. Tools and Materials: IIc. Carved Sculpture. *Am Mag of Art* 28:156-60 Mr 1935. 2 il.

16. Views and Methods. *Creative Art* 6:443-5 Je 1930. 3 il.

17. Where is Sculpture Today? *College Art Journal* 16:329-31 Summer 1957. 2 il.

18. *Zorach Explains Sculpture*, 1947. 302p 300 il.

BOOKS AND EXHIBITION CATALOGUES

19. Agard, Walter Raymond: *The New Architectural Sculpture*, 1935, p 52.

20. [*The Armory Show.*] *International Exhibition of Modern Art*, N. Y., 1913.

20a Art Students League, N. Y.: *William Zorach*, 1950. 20p 12 il.

21. Baur, John I. H.: *Revolution and Tradition in Modern American Art*, Cambridge, 1951, p36, 48,56,57,58,61,75,95. 2 il.

22. Bryant, Lorinda Munson: *American Pictures and Their Painters*, 1920, p298-9. 1 il.

23. Cahill, Holger: "American Art Today" in *America as Americans See It*, Fred J. Ringel, ed., 1932, p254,260,264.

24. Cahill, Holger, and Barr, Alfred H., Jr., ed.: *Art in America in Modern Times*, 1934, p37, 56-7. 1 il.

25. Cheney, Martha Candler: *Modern Art in America*, 1939, p69-70,154-5,161. 1 il.

26. *Current Biography*, 1943, p854-6. 1 il.

27. Downtown Gallery, N.Y.: *William Zorach*, Foreword by Holger Cahill, 1931. 5p 4 il.

28. *Forum Exhibition of Modern American Painters*, N. Y., 1916. 1 il.

29. LaFollette, Suzanne: *Art in America*, 1929, p333, 343.

30. Larkin, Oliver W.: *Art and Life in America*, 1949, p395,442. 1 il.

31. Moore, Dorothy Lefferts: "A Note on William Zorach" in *The Arts Portfolio Series*, Forbes Watson, ed., 1931. 12 pl.

32. Museum of Modern Art, N. Y.: *American Painting & Sculpture*, 1932, pl9,21. 1 il.

33. ——— *Art in Our Time*, 1939. 2 il.

34. ——— *Painting and Sculpture by Living Americans*, 1930. 1 il.

34a *National Encyclopedia*, V. 9 [1933], p115-21.

35. Parkes, Kineton: *The Art of Carved Sculpture*, London, 1931, V. I, p150-3. 1 il.

36. Phillips, Duncan: *A Collection in the Making*, 1926, p71. 1 il.

37. Ritchie, Andrew Carnduff: *Sculpture of the Twentieth Century*, 1952, p20-1. 1 il.

38. Schnier, Jacques: *Sculpture in Modern America*, Los Angeles, 1948, p22. 3 il.

39. Whitney Museum of American Art, N.Y.: *Pioneers of Modern Art in America*, 1946. 1 il.

40. Wingert, Paul S.: *The Sculpture of William Zorach*, 1938. 74p 50 il.

41. *William Zorach*, American Artists Group, 1945. [16]p 48 il. Reprinted from bibl 3.

PERIODICALS

42. American Says Soviet "Stole" Idea for Huge Palace. *Newsweek* 3:15 Mr 17 1934. 2 il.

43. Art Comes to Palm Beach. *Time* 38:40 Jl 7 1941. 1 il.

44. Books. Reviews & Comments. *Art Digest* 13:31 N 15 1938.

45. Bookshelf. *Art News* 47:51 Mr 1948.

46. Bowdoin College Presents Honorary Degree to William Zorach. *Art Students League News* 11:1 S 1958.

47. Brenner, Anita: Zorach and Modern Art. *Menorah Journal* 16:322-4 Ap 1929. 8 il.

48. Breuning, Margaret: Sculptor Zorach Shows Swift Watercolors. *Art Digest* 18:14 My 15 1944. 1 il.

49. —— Zorach Milestone. *Art Digest* 25:16 N 15 1950. 1 il.

50. A.v.C.: The Zorachs at Daniels. *Am Art News* 14:5 D 4 1915.

51. Cary, Elizabeth Luther: Modern American Prints. *International Studio* 80:218-19 D 1924. 1 il.

52. A Cast Lady Cast Off. *Life* 41:93-4 Jl 23 1956. 3 il.

53. Chicago's Annual Draws Eyes of Fighters for American Art. *Art Digest* 6:3-4 N 1 1931. 1 il.

54. Coates, Robert M.: The Art Galleries. *New Yorker* 20:68-9 My 27 1944.

55. —— 23:92-3 Mr. 15, 1947.

56. —— 27:99 Mr 3 1951.

57. Cole, Mary: Modern Humanism. *Art Digest* 25:15 Mr 1 1951. 1 il.

58. Glenn Coleman and the Zorachs. *Am Art News* 15:2 N 11 1916.

59. "Continuity Between Tradition and Today." *Art Digest* 5:12 F 1 1931. 2 il.

60. Cross, Louise: William Zorach. *London Studio* 8:80-2 Ag 1934. 3 il.

61. Dahlov. *Time* 34:52 N 13 1939. 3 il.

62. Danes, Gibson: William Zorach [In "Book Reviews."] *Mag of Art* 41:243-4 O 1948.

63. Dean of Sculptors. *Time* 67:84 Je 11 1956. 1 il.

64. Denver Dispute. *Art Digest* 11:15 O 1 1936.

65. Exhibitions in New York. *Art News* 31:9 Ja 7 1933.

66. Exit the "Faun Era." *Art Digest* 12:21 O 1 1937.

67. Female Figure by Zorach. *Vanity Fair* 33:60-1 N 1929. 2 il.

68. Field Notes. Will Texas Miss? *Am Mag of Art* 29:362,413,415-16 Je 1936. 1 il.

69. Flint, Ralph: Zorach's Work at Downtown Galleries. *Art News* 29:6 Ja 31 1931.

70. The Forty-fourth Annual at Chicago. *Am Mag of Art* 23:487-8 D 1931. 1 il.

71. Frost, Rosamund: Guilded Sculptors Show. *Art News* 37:6-7 0 22, 1938. 1 il.

72. C.A.G.: Around the Galleries. *Creative Art* 10: 228-9 Mr 1932. 1 il.

73. B.H.: William Zorach. [In "Reviews and Previews."] *Art News* 50:49 Mr 1951. 1 il.

74. Heineberg, Dora Jane: The Technique of Wood Sculpture Demonstrated by William Zorach. *Parnassus* 13:107-10 Mr 1941. 11 il.

75. Honor Goes to Zorach at Chicago Water Color International. *Art Digest* 6:5 Ap 1 1932. 1 il.

76. Hudnut, Joseph: Contemporary Sculpture. *Fairmount Park Art Association 61st Annual Report* p26,29,33,35,37 1933. 2 il.

77. Kellow, F. L.: Zorach's Sculpture. *Survey* 66:40-1 Ap 1 1931. 4 il.

78. Knowlton, Walter: Around the Galleries. *Creative Art* 8:sup84-5,90 Mr 1931. 1 il.

79. Krasne, Belle: A Zorach Profile. *Art Digest* 26:5, 26 N 15 1951. 1 il.

80. M.L.: Zorach Watercolors [In "Fifty-seventh Street in Review."] *Art Digest* 23:21-2 D 15 1948. 1 il.

81. Lansford, Alonzo: Zorach Continues to Add to His Fame. *Art Digest* 21:13 Mr 15 1947. 1 il.

82. M.M.: William Zorach [In "Exhibitions."] *International Studio* 98:74 Mr 1931.

83. McMahon, A. Philip: New Books on Art. *Parnassus* 11:31 F 1939.

84. Monumental Coincidence. *Architectural Forum* 60:sup22 Ap 1934. 1 il.

85. New Books on Art. *Mag of Art* 31:428 Jl 1938.

86. New York Criticism. *Art Digest* 6:19 F 15 1932.

87. New York Season. *Art Digest* 5:14 F 15 1931.

88. Page, A. F.: A Terra Cotta by William Zorach. *Detroit Institute of Arts Bul* 30no1:19-21 1950-51. 1 il.

89. The Passing Shows. *Art News* 42:24 Mr 15 1943. 1 il.

90. —— 43:21 My 15 1944.

91. Possibly Eternal. *Time* 60:84 D 15 1952. 1 il.

92. Recent and Current Exhibitions in New York. *Parnassus* 3:15,49 F 1931.

93. Reed, Judith Kaye: Art Book Library. *Art Digest* 22:29 F 1 1948.

94. Reviews and Previews. *Art News* 46:22-3 Mr 1947. 1 il.

95. —— 47:50 D 1948.

96. Riley, Maude: Carvings by Zorach. *Art Digest* 17:7 Mr 1 1943. 1 il.

97. Roberts, Mary Fanton: Speaking of Art. *Arts & Decoration* 34:80 Mr 1931.

98. Ronnebeck and Zorach Storm Centers in Tempest Over Statue. *Art Digest* 10:8-9 S 1 1936. 1 il.

99. Sayre, Ann H.: Maine Watercolors by a Living Sculptor In ["New Exhibitions of the Week."] *Art News* 34:8 Mr 7 1936. 1 il.

100. Sculpture in Silver. *Am Artist* 19:49,69 N 1955. 1 il.

101. Sculpture Lesson. *Life* 24:75-9 My 31 1948. 13 il.

102. Sculptures by William Zorach. *Vanity Fair* 32:45 Jl 1929. 4 il.

103. A Season for Sculpture. *Arts* 30:23 Ja 1956. 1 il.

104. Slusser, Jean Paul: Modernistic Pictures Done in Wool. *Arts & Decoration* 18:30 Ja 1923. 3 il.

105. Smith, Jacob Getlar: Another Side to William Zorach. *Am Artist* 22:20-7,57. 13 il.

106. The Speer Memorial. *Mag of Art* 30:172-3 Mr 1937. 5 il.

107. Strawn, Arthur: The Zorachs. *Outlook* 157:236 F 11 1931.

108. Texas Insists That Its Pioneers Be Clothed and Decent. *Newsweek* 7:48 Ap 18 1936. 1 il.

109. Three to Start '56. *Art News* 54:37, 59-60 Ja 1956. 1 il.

110. "Tooky" Is Taken. *Art Digest* 11:26 Ag 1 1937. 1 il.

111. Turner, G. Alan: William Zorach. *Design* 52:8-9 Ap 1951. 7 il.

112. Villard, Mariquita: William Zorach and His Sculpture. *Parnassus* 6:3-6 0 1934. 3 il.

113. Watercolors of All Nations. *Art News* 37:12 0 22 1938. 1 il.

114. Watson, Forbes: New York Exhibitions. *Arts* 13: 188, 191-2 Mr 1928. 1 il.

115. Werner, Alfred: Art. *Frontier* 7:22 Mr 1956.

116. What Is Art in the Face of Texas Modesty? *Art Digest* 10:6 My 1 1936. 1 il.

117. Wheelock, Warren: William Zorach. *Art Instruction* 3:18-21 Ap 1939. 4 il.

118. Would Nude Statues, Pure as a Dew-Drop, Debauch Roxy's "Public"? *Art Digest* 7:7,20 Ja 1 1933. 1 il.

119. Zorach. *Life* 8:90-3 Ap 1 1940. 7 il.

120. Zorach, Great Water Colorist. *Art Digest* 10:16 Mr 15 1936.

121. Zorach Panels Rejected by Texas Bank. *Architectural Forum* 105:25 Jl 1956. 1 il.

122. William Zorach: Downtown Gallery. *Art News* 30:11 Ja 30 1932.

123. William Zorach—Sculptor. *Index of Twentieth Century Artists* 1no8:124-6 sup i, iii, vi My 1934.

124. Zorach's Heroic New Statue. *Vanity Fair* 36:54 Mr 1931. 2 il.

125. Zorach's Old Role. *Art Digest* 10:24 Mr 1 1936.

126. The Zorachs at Daniel Gallery. *Am Art News* 16:3 Mr 23 1918.

127. Zorach's Recent Work. *Am Art News* 17:3 Mr 29 1919.

Index